Introduction to Workplace Investigations

by

Aaron Bucy

Island Entertainment Media

Sherman, Texas

ISBN: 978-1-7320802-2-5

Produced and Distributed by Island Entertainment Media

Printed in the United States of America

First Edition

16 15 14 13 12 11 10 /10 9 8 7 6 5 4 3 2 1

Library of Congress Control Number: TBD

Island Entertainment Media, Sherman, Texas

Table Of Contents

Why Companies Conduct Workplace Investigations

Workplace investigations are an important tool for companies to ensure a safe, fair, and productive work environment for all employees. They are used to address a wide range of issues, including harassment, discrimination, fraud, violence, and ethical misconduct. By conducting investigations, companies can identify and address problems early on, before they escalate and cause significant harm to the organization or its employees.

There are many reasons why companies choose to conduct investigations. One of the most important is to protect the company's reputation and brand. Companies that are known for their commitment to fairness, integrity, and respect are more likely to attract and retain the best employees and customers. Additionally, investigations can help companies avoid costly lawsuits, government fines, and negative publicity.

Another key reason for conducting investigations is to ensure compliance with federal and state laws. Many laws, such as Title VII of the Civil Rights Act and the Americans with Disabilities Act, require employers to take steps to prevent and address discrimination and harassment in the workplace. By conducting investigations, companies can demonstrate their commitment to compliance and reduce their risk of legal action.

Investigations also serve an important role in maintaining a positive work culture and fostering an environment where employees feel safe, respected, and valued. When employees feel that their concerns are taken seriously and that appropriate action will be taken to address them, they are more likely to be engaged, productive, and committed to the company.

In summary, workplace investigations are a critical tool for companies to maintain a safe, fair, and productive work environment, protect their reputation and brand, ensure compliance with laws, and foster a positive work culture. They are an important part of an organization's overall risk management strategy, and can help companies avoid costly legal action and negative publicity.

The History of Workplace Investigations

The concept of workplace investigations has a long and storied history, dating back to the early days of the industrial revolution. As factories and businesses began to proliferate in the late 19th and early 20th centuries, so too did concerns about the treatment of workers and the safety of the workplace.

In response to these concerns, various laws and regulations were put into place to protect workers and ensure that they were treated fairly. Some of the earliest workplace investigations were conducted by government agencies, such as the Occupational Safety and Health Administration (OSHA) and the National Labor Relations Board (NLRB). These investigations were often focused on issues such as safety hazards, discrimination, and union-busting.

As the 20th century progressed, the scope of workplace investigations began to broaden. More and more companies began to conduct internal investigations in response to allegations of misconduct or illegal activity. These investigations were often conducted by in-house legal teams or outside consultants, and they were typically focused on issues such as embezzlement, fraud, and harassment.

In recent years, the importance of workplace investigations has only grown. With the rise of the #MeToo movement and increased awareness of workplace discrimination and harassment, more and more companies are taking proactive steps to address these issues. Additionally, with the increased focus on corporate governance and compliance, many companies are now conducting investigations as a matter of course in order to protect themselves from legal liability.

Despite the long history of workplace investigations, the field is constantly evolving. As new laws and regulations are put into place, and as new issues and challenges arise, the nature of workplace investigations will continue to change. Nevertheless, the core goal of workplace investigations – to ensure that workplaces are safe, fair, and compliant – will always remain the same.

One example of a famous workplace investigation is the investigation into the sexual harassment allegations against Hollywood producer Harvey Weinstein. In 2017, multiple women came forward with allegations of sexual harassment and assault against Weinstein, leading to an investigation by the New York Police Department and the Manhattan District Attorney's office. The investigation resulted in Weinstein being charged with multiple counts of sexual assault and rape, and he was ultimately convicted and sentenced to 23 years in prison. The case led to a significant increase in the number of workplace harassment and assault allegations being reported and brought attention to the issue of sexual misconduct in the entertainment industry and beyond.

The Google Walkout: In 2018, thousands of Google employees around the world walked out of their offices to protest the company's handling of sexual harassment and misconduct allegations. The walkout was sparked by an article in The New York Times that revealed that Google had protected several high-ranking executives from being fired despite credible allegations of misconduct. The walkout led to an internal investigation, which found that Google had mishandled several harassment and misconduct claims. As a result, the company made changes to its policies and procedures for handling such allegations, including the creation of an employee representative on the board and a commitment to being more transparent about such issues.

The Wells Fargo Scandal: In 2016, Wells Fargo was investigated by several government agencies, including the Consumer Financial Protection Bureau and the Office of the Comptroller of the Currency, after it was revealed that employees had opened millions of unauthorized accounts in order to meet sales goals. The investigation found that the bank's high-pressure sales culture had led to widespread unethical and illegal behavior, and Wells Fargo agreed to pay $185 million in fines and settlements. The bank also implemented a number of reforms, including an overhaul of its sales practices and the creation of a new position of chief risk officer, as well as the firing of several high-ranking executives.

CHAPTER 1

Overview of Workplace Investigations

What is a workplace investigation?

A workplace investigation is a process of gathering and evaluating information in order to determine whether or not an incident or complaint has occurred and, if so, what actions should be taken to address it. Workplace investigations can be conducted for a variety of reasons, including allegations of harassment, discrimination, fraud, embezzlement, workplace violence, and ethical misconduct.

Why are workplace investigations important?

Workplace investigations serve several important functions. They help employers to identify and address problems that can negatively impact the workplace and its employees. They also help employers to comply with laws and regulations that prohibit harassment, discrimination, and other forms of misconduct. Additionally, investigations can help to promote transparency, accountability, and fairness in the workplace.

Who conducts workplace investigations?

Workplace investigations can be conducted by a variety of individuals or entities, including internal HR representatives, external investigators, attorneys, or other professionals with relevant expertise. The specific individuals or entities that conduct investigations will vary depending on the circumstances and the nature of the complaint or incident.

How are workplace investigations conducted?

The specific steps and processes involved in conducting a workplace investigation will vary depending on the circumstances and the nature of the complaint or incident. However, investigations typically involve the following steps: planning and preparation, conducting the investigation, making findings and recommendations, and concluding the investigation.

Challenges in workplace investigations

Conducting a thorough and fair investigation can be challenging, particularly when the investigation involves sensitive or controversial issues. Some of the common challenges that investigators may face include resistance or obstruction from employees or management, conflicting witness statements, and lack of cooperation or access to key evidence. Additionally, legal and ethical considerations can also add complexity to the investigation process.

Conclusion

Workplace investigations are an important tool for employers to identify and address problems that can negatively impact the workplace and its employees. Understanding the basics of workplace investigations, including their purpose, how they are conducted, and the challenges involved, is crucial for anyone who may be called upon to conduct or participate in an investigation.

CHAPTER 2

Purpose of the Training Book

Introduction

This training book is designed to provide an overview of the key concepts and best practices related to workplace investigations. It is intended to serve as a resource for anyone who may be called upon to conduct or participate in an investigation, including HR representatives, managers, supervisors, and other professionals.

Objectives

The primary objectives of this training book are to:

1. Provide an overview of the legal and regulatory requirements governing workplace investigations.
2. Explain the different types of workplace investigations and the specific considerations involved in each.
3. Provide guidance on planning and conducting effective workplace investigations.
4. Explain how to make findings and recommendations based on the evidence gathered during the investigation.
5. Provide strategies for communicating findings and implementing corrective action.

Audience

This training book is intended for a wide range of professionals, including:

- Human resources representatives and managers
- Supervisors and managers
- Legal and compliance professionals
- Internal and external investigators
- Attorneys and other legal professionals

Format

This book is divided into chapters, each covering a specific topic related to workplace investigations. Each chapter includes a summary of key concepts, practical examples, and recommended best practices.

Conclusion

This training book is designed to provide a comprehensive overview of the key concepts and best practices related to workplace investigations. By understanding the legal and regulatory requirements, the different types of investigations and how to conduct them effectively, the audience of this book will be able to handle workplace investigations with confidence, fairness, and professionalism.

CHAPTER 3

Audience for this Book

Introduction

This book is designed for a wide range of professionals who may be called upon to conduct or participate in workplace investigations. Understanding the key concepts and best practices related to workplace investigations is crucial for anyone in these roles, as they play an important role in ensuring a safe, fair, and compliant workplace.

Human Resources Professionals

Human resources (HR) professionals are often the first point of contact for employees who want to report incidents or complaints of misconduct. As such, they play a critical role in ensuring that investigations are conducted in a timely, thorough, and fair manner. This training book is designed to provide HR professionals with the knowledge and skills they need to conduct effective workplace investigations, including understanding legal and regulatory requirements, planning and conducting investigations, and communicating findings and implementing corrective action.

Managers and Supervisors

Managers and supervisors also play an important role in conducting workplace investigations. They may be responsible for conducting investigations, supervising investigations conducted by others, or making decisions based on the findings of investigations. This training book is designed to provide managers and supervisors with the knowledge and skills they need to conduct effective workplace investigations, including understanding legal and regulatory requirements, identifying and addressing misconduct, and communicating findings and implementing corrective action.

Legal and Compliance Professionals

Legal and compliance professionals play a critical role in ensuring that investigations are conducted in compliance with relevant laws and regulations. This training book is designed to provide legal and compliance professionals with the knowledge and skills they need to conduct effective workplace investigations, including understanding legal and regulatory requirements, identifying and addressing misconduct, and communicating findings and implementing corrective action.

Internal and External Investigators

Internal and external investigators play a critical role in conducting workplace investigations. They are responsible for gathering and evaluating evidence, interviewing witnesses, and making findings and recommendations based on their findings. This training book is designed to provide investigators with the knowledge and skills they need to conduct effective workplace investigations, including understanding legal and regulatory requirements, identifying and addressing misconduct, and communicating findings and implementing corrective action.

Conclusion

This training book is designed to provide a wide range of professionals with the knowledge and skills they need to conduct effective workplace investigations. By understanding the legal and regulatory requirements, the different types of investigations and how to conduct them effectively, the audience of this book will be able to handle workplace investigations with confidence, fairness and professionalism.

CHAPTER 4

Federal and State Laws Governing Workplace Investigations

Introduction

Workplace investigations are governed by a variety of federal and state laws, which set out the legal requirements for conducting investigations and provide protections for employees and employers. Understanding these laws is essential for anyone who may be called upon to conduct or participate in a workplace investigation.

Federal Laws

Title VII of the Civil Rights Act of 1964: Title VII prohibits discrimination on the basis of race, color, sex, national origin, and religion. Employers are required to take prompt and appropriate action to investigate and remedy discrimination complaints.

The Americans with Disabilities Act (ADA): The ADA prohibits discrimination on the basis of disability. Employers are required to make reasonable accommodations for employees with disabilities, and to investigate and remedy discrimination complaints.

The Age Discrimination in Employment Act (ADEA): The ADEA prohibits discrimination on the basis of age. Employers are required to investigate and remedy discrimination complaints.

The Family and Medical Leave Act (FMLA): The FMLA guarantees eligible employees up to 12 weeks of unpaid leave for certain family and medical reasons. Employers are required to investigate and remedy complaints of interference with FMLA rights.

The National Labor Relations Act (NLRA): The NLRA guarantees employees the right to form, join, or assist labor organizations, and to engage in protected concerted activities. Employers are required to investigate and remedy complaints of unfair labor practices.

State Laws

State discrimination laws: Many states have their own discrimination laws that provide additional protections for employees. Employers are required to comply with both federal and state discrimination laws.

State whistleblower protection laws: Many states have laws that protect employees who report misconduct from retaliation. Employers are required to comply with these laws and investigate complaints of retaliation.

State wage and hour laws: Many states have laws that set out the legal requirements for minimum wage, overtime, and other wage and hour issues. Employers are required to comply with these laws and investigate complaints of wage and hour violations.

Conclusion

Workplace investigations are governed by a variety of federal and state laws, which set out the legal requirements for conducting investigations and provide protections for employees and employers. Understanding these laws is essential for anyone who may be called upon to conduct or participate in a workplace investigation. Employers are required to comply with these laws and investigate complaints of misconduct, discrimination, and retaliation. It is important to consult with legal counsel when conducting investigations to ensure compliance with all relevant laws and regulations.

CHAPTER 5

Tribal and Native American Workplace Investigations

The unique cultural and legal landscape of tribal and Native American workplaces can create additional challenges when conducting investigations. These challenges include:

- **Sovereignty**: Many tribes have their own legal systems and courts, which can make it difficult to navigate issues related to jurisdiction and authority.
- **Tribal customs and traditions**: Tribal cultures and traditions can play a significant role in workplace dynamics and can impact the way in which investigations are conducted.
- **Limited resources**: Many tribal and Native American workplaces have limited resources, which can make it difficult to conduct investigations in a thorough and professional manner.

Despite these challenges, it is important to remember that all employees, regardless of their cultural background, have the right to work in a safe and discrimination-free environment. Therefore, it is essential to ensure that tribal and Native American workplaces are held to the same standards as other workplaces when it comes to conducting investigations.

Best practices for conducting investigations in tribal and Native American workplaces include:

- **Building relationships and trust with tribal leaders and community members**: It is essential to establish a positive relationship with tribal leaders and community members to ensure a smooth and effective investigation.
- **Providing cultural sensitivity training**: It is important to ensure that investigators are trained to understand and respect the cultural customs and traditions of the tribe or Native American community.
- **Utilizing local resources**: Utilizing local resources such as tribal police, legal counsel, and community advocates can be helpful in navigating the unique challenges of tribal and Native American workplaces.
- **Being aware of and respectful of the tribe's or Native American community's sovereignty**: It is important to be aware of and respectful of the tribe's or Native American community's sovereignty when conducting investigations.

Conducting investigations in tribal and Native American workplaces can be challenging due to the unique cultural and legal landscape. However, by building relationships and trust, providing cultural sensitivity training, utilizing local resources, and being aware of and respectful of sovereignty, investigations can be conducted in a thorough and professional manner to ensure a safe and discrimination-free work environment for all employees.

CHAPTER 6

Best Practices for Compliance

Introduction

Compliance with legal and regulatory requirements is a critical aspect of conducting effective workplace investigations. Best practices for compliance include clearly understanding the legal and regulatory requirements, developing and implementing policies and procedures, and training employees on their rights and responsibilities.

Understanding Legal and Regulatory Requirements

- Familiarize yourself with the relevant federal and state laws and regulations that apply to your organization and the specific investigation you are conducting.
- Seek legal counsel as needed to ensure compliance with all relevant laws and regulations.
- Review and update your organization's policies and procedures as necessary to ensure compliance with legal and regulatory requirements.

Developing and Implementing Policies and Procedures

- Develop and implement clear and comprehensive policies and procedures for conducting workplace investigations.
- Ensure that your policies and procedures are consistent with legal and regulatory requirements and best practices.

- Communicate your policies and procedures to all employees and provide training on their rights and responsibilities.
- Regularly review and update your policies and procedures as necessary to ensure ongoing compliance.

Training Employees

- Provide regular training for employees on legal and regulatory requirements, as well as the organization's policies and procedures for conducting workplace investigations.
- Train employees on their rights and responsibilities in the event of a workplace investigation.
- Train managers and supervisors on their responsibilities in conducting investigations and ensuring compliance with legal and regulatory requirements.

Summary

Compliance with legal and regulatory requirements is a critical aspect of conducting effective workplace investigations. By understanding the legal and regulatory requirements, developing and implementing policies and procedures, and training employees on their rights and responsibilities, organizations can ensure compliance and protect the rights of all employees. It is important to regularly review and update policies and procedures to ensure ongoing compliance.

CHAPTER 7

Common Legal Pitfalls to Avoid

Introduction
Workplace investigations can be complex and legally sensitive, and it is important to be aware of common legal pitfalls to avoid. Failure to comply with legal and regulatory requirements, or to follow best practices can result in legal liability for the organization and individuals involved in the investigation.

Failure to Investigate
Failure to investigate a complaint or report of misconduct or discrimination can result in legal liability for the organization. Failure to take prompt and appropriate action to investigate can also result in liability, particularly in cases of discrimination or harassment.

Failure to Follow Due Process
Failure to provide employees with due process during an investigation can result in legal liability for the organization. Due process includes providing employees with notice of the allegations against them, the opportunity to respond, and a fair and impartial investigation.

Failure to Keep the Investigation Confidential
Failure to keep the investigation confidential can result in legal liability for the organization and individuals involved in the investigation. Confidentiality is important to protect the rights of

all parties involved in the investigation, and to maintain the integrity of the investigation.

Retaliating Against Complainants or Witnesses

Retaliating against complainants or witnesses can result in legal liability for the organization and individuals involved. Retaliation includes any adverse action taken against an employee in response to their participation in an investigation, including termination, demotion, or disciplinary action.

Failure to Provide Adequate Remedies

Failure to provide adequate remedies for misconduct or discrimination can result in legal liability for the organization. Adequate remedies include taking appropriate disciplinary action against individuals found to have engaged in misconduct or discrimination, and implementing measures to prevent future misconduct or discrimination.

Conclusion

Workplace investigations can be complex and legally sensitive, and it is important to be aware of common legal pitfalls to avoid. Failure to comply with legal and regulatory requirements or to follow best practices can result in legal liability for the organization and individuals involved in the investigation. It is important to conduct investigations in a fair, impartial, and confidential manner, to provide due process to all parties involved, and to take appropriate action in response to misconduct or discrimination. It is also important to seek legal counsel as needed to ensure compliance with all relevant laws and regulations.

CHAPTER 8

Harassment and Discrimination Investigations

Introduction

Harassment and discrimination investigations are a crucial aspect of maintaining a safe and inclusive workplace. It is important for organizations to have policies and procedures in place to address and investigate complaints of harassment and discrimination, and to take appropriate action in response to any violations.

Defining Harassment and Discrimination

- Harassment is defined as unwanted or unwelcome conduct that is based on a protected characteristic, such as race, sex, age, religion, or disability.
- Discrimination is defined as treating an individual differently or less favorably based on a protected characteristic.

Protected characteristics vary by jurisdiction, but commonly include race, sex, age, religion, national origin, disability, sexual orientation, and gender identity.

Investigating Harassment and Discrimination Complaints

Organizations should have policies and procedures in place for employees to report complaints of harassment and discrimination.

The investigation process should be prompt, impartial, and thorough, and should include interviewing the complainant, the alleged harasser, and any witnesses. The investigation should be conducted by a trained and impartial investigator, and all parties should be provided with due process. The investigation should be kept confidential to the extent possible, to protect the rights of all parties involved.

Responding to Harassment and Discrimination

If the investigation finds that harassment or discrimination has occurred, appropriate action should be taken in response. This may include disciplinary action against the individual(s) found to have engaged in harassment or discrimination, as well as measures to prevent future incidents, such as training and education for employees.

Organizations should also take steps to ensure that complainants are protected from retaliation.

Summary

Harassment and discrimination investigations are a crucial aspect of maintaining a safe and inclusive workplace. It is important for organizations to have policies and procedures in place to address and investigate complaints of harassment and discrimination, and to take appropriate action in response to any violations. The investigation process should be prompt, impartial, and thorough, and should include interviewing the complainant, the alleged harasser, and any witnesses. It is also important to keep the investigation confidential to the extent possible, to protect the rights of all parties involved. Organizations should also take steps to ensure that complainants are protected from retaliation.

CHAPTER 9

Fraud and Embezzlement Investigations

Introduction

Fraud and embezzlement investigations are an important aspect of preventing and detecting financial misconduct within organizations. These investigations can be complex and require specialized knowledge and skills to conduct.

Defining Fraud and Embezzlement

- Fraud is defined as the intentional deception or misrepresentation of facts for the purpose of financial gain.
- Embezzlement is defined as the unauthorized use or misappropriation of funds or assets for personal gain.

Both fraud and embezzlement can take many forms, including financial statement fraud, asset misappropriation, and bribery.

Investigating Fraud and Embezzlement

Organizations should have policies and procedures in place for employees to report suspicions of fraud and embezzlement. The investigation process should be prompt, thorough, and conducted by trained professionals with knowledge and experience in fraud and embezzlement investigations. The investigation should include a review of financial records and documents, as well as interviews with relevant parties. The investigation should be conducted in a confidential manner to protect the rights of all parties involved and to maintain the integrity of the investigation.

Responding to Fraud and Embezzlement

If the investigation finds evidence of fraud or embezzlement, appropriate action should be taken in response. This may include disciplinary action against the individual(s) found to have engaged in fraud or embezzlement, as well as measures to prevent future incidents, such as improved internal controls and financial reporting systems. Depending on the outcome of the investigation, legal action may also be taken against the individual(s) involved.

Conclusion

Fraud and embezzlement investigations are an important aspect of preventing and detecting financial misconduct within organizations. These investigations can be complex and require specialized knowledge and skills to conduct. Organizations should have policies and procedures in place for employees to report suspicions of fraud and embezzlement, and the investigation process should be prompt, thorough and conducted by trained professionals with knowledge and experience in fraud and embezzlement investigations. It is important to maintain the confidentiality of the investigation process to protect the rights of all parties involved and maintain the integrity of the investigation. Organizations should take appropriate actions based on the outcome of the investigation, including disciplinary actions, implementing measures to prevent future incidents and legal actions if needed.

CHAPTER 10

Workplace Violence and Threat Investigations

Introduction

Workplace violence and threat investigations are important aspects of maintaining a safe and secure working environment for employees. These investigations can be complex and require specialized knowledge and skills to conduct.

Defining Workplace Violence and Threats

- Workplace violence is defined as any physical or verbal act that can cause harm or injury to an employee while on the job.
- Threats are defined as any verbal or written statement that can cause fear or concern for an employee's safety while on the job.

Both workplace violence and threats can take many forms, including physical attacks, verbal abuse, and stalking.

Investigating Workplace Violence and Threats

Organizations should have policies and procedures in place for employees to report suspicions of workplace violence and threats. The investigation process should be prompt, thorough, and conducted by trained professionals with knowledge and experience in workplace violence and threat investigations. The investigation should include a review of any available evidence, as well as interviews with relevant parties. The investigation should be conducted in a confidential manner to protect the rights of all parties involved and to maintain the integrity of the investigation.

Responding to Workplace Violence and Threats

If the investigation finds evidence of workplace violence or threats, appropriate action should be taken in response. This may include disciplinary action against the individual(s) found to have engaged in workplace violence or made threats, as well as measures to prevent future incidents, such as improved security and employee training programs. Depending on the outcome of the investigation, legal action may also be taken against the individual(s) involved.

Conclusion

Workplace violence and threat investigations are important aspects of maintaining a safe and secure working environment for employees. These investigations can be complex and require specialized knowledge and skills to conduct. Organizations should have policies and procedures in place for employees to report suspicions of workplace violence and threats, and the investigation process should be prompt, thorough, and conducted by trained professionals with knowledge and experience in workplace violence and threat investigations. It is important to maintain the confidentiality of the investigation process to protect the rights of all parties involved and maintain the integrity of the investigation. Organizations should take appropriate actions based on the outcome of the investigation, including disciplinary actions, implementing measures to prevent future incidents and legal actions if needed.

CHAPTER 11

Ethical Misconduct Investigations

Introduction
Ethical misconduct investigations are an important aspect of maintaining a culture of integrity and accountability within an organization. These investigations can be complex and require specialized knowledge and skills to conduct.

Defining Ethical Misconduct
Ethical misconduct refers to any behavior that violates an organization's code of conduct or ethical standards. This can include issues such as conflicts of interest, fraud, embezzlement, bribery, and insider trading. Ethical misconduct can also include issues such as sexual harassment, discrimination, and retaliation.

Investigating Ethical Misconduct
Organizations should have policies and procedures in place for employees to report suspicions of ethical misconduct. The investigation process should be prompt, thorough, and conducted by trained professionals with knowledge and experience in ethical misconduct investigations. The investigation should include a review of any available evidence, as well as interviews with relevant parties. The investigation should be conducted in a confidential manner to protect the rights of all parties involved and to maintain the integrity of the investigation.

Responding to Ethical Misconduct

If the investigation finds evidence of ethical misconduct, appropriate action should be taken in response. This may include disciplinary action against the individual(s) found to have engaged in ethical misconduct, as well as measures to prevent future incidents, such as improved compliance and employee training programs. Depending on the outcome of the investigation, legal action may also be taken against the individual(s) involved.

Conclusion

Ethical misconduct investigations are an important aspect of maintaining a culture of integrity and accountability within an organization. These investigations can be complex and require specialized knowledge and skills to conduct. Organizations should have policies and procedures in place for employees to report suspicions of ethical misconduct, and the investigation process should be prompt, thorough, and conducted by trained professionals with knowledge and experience in ethical misconduct investigations. It is important to maintain the confidentiality of the investigation process to protect the rights of all parties involved and maintain the integrity of the investigation. Organizations should take appropriate actions based on the outcome of the investigation, including disciplinary actions, implementing measures to prevent future incidents and legal actions if needed.

CHAPTER 12

Identifying the Scope of the Investigation

Introduction

When a workplace investigation is launched, it's important to clearly define the scope of the investigation. This means determining what specific issues or behaviors are being investigated and who is involved. Having a clear scope will help ensure that the investigation is thorough and focused, and that it addresses all the relevant concerns.

Determining the Issues at Hand

The first step in identifying the scope of the investigation is to determine what specific issues or behaviors are being investigated. This could be anything from allegations of harassment or discrimination, to suspicions of fraud or embezzlement. It's important to gather as much information as possible about the allegations, including any relevant documents or evidence, as well as statements from the individuals involved.

Identifying the Parties Involved

Once the issues at hand have been identified, it's important to determine who is involved in the investigation. This may include the person making the allegations, any witnesses, and the person or persons against whom the allegations have been made. It's also important to consider any other parties who may be impacted by the investigation, such as co-workers or supervisors, and to include them in the scope of the investigation if necessary.

Setting the Timeframe

Another important aspect of identifying the scope of the investigation is determining the timeframe of the events in question. This will help to establish a clear timeline of events and ensure that any relevant evidence is not overlooked. It's important to consider events that occurred both before and after the specific incident or incidents being investigated, as they may be relevant to the investigation.

Conclusion

Clearly defining the scope of a workplace investigation is crucial to ensuring that the investigation is thorough and focused. This includes determining the specific issues or behaviors being investigated, identifying the parties involved, and establishing a clear timeline of events. By taking the time to properly identify the scope of the investigation, organizations can ensure that all relevant concerns are addressed, and that a fair and impartial investigation is conducted.

CHAPTER 13

Identifying and Selecting Investigators

Introduction
When it comes to workplace investigations, selecting the right investigator is crucial. The investigator is responsible for conducting a fair and impartial investigation, and their credibility and qualifications can greatly impact the outcome of the investigation.

Qualifications of an Investigator
The first step in identifying and selecting investigators is to consider their qualifications. This may include their education, experience, and professional certifications. It's important to select investigators who have experience in the specific area of the investigation, such as harassment or discrimination, fraud or embezzlement, or workplace violence. It's also important to ensure that the investigator has knowledge of the relevant laws and regulations, such as those governing workplace investigations.

Independence and Impartiality
Another important factor to consider when selecting investigators is their independence and impartiality. The investigator should not have any conflicts of interest that could compromise the integrity of the investigation. It's important to ensure that the investigator is not connected to any of the parties involved in the investigation

and that they do not have any personal or professional relationships that could be perceived as a conflict of interest.

Communication and Interpersonal Skills

Strong communication and interpersonal skills are also important when selecting investigators. The investigator should be able to effectively communicate with all parties involved in the investigation and to gather information in a professional and respectful manner.

It's also important that the investigator is able to present their findings in a clear and concise manner, both verbally and in writing.

Conclusion

Selecting the right investigator is crucial to the success of a workplace investigation. Qualifications, independence, impartiality, and strong communication and interpersonal skills are all important factors to consider when identifying and selecting investigators. By taking the time to carefully select investigators who possess these qualities, organizations can ensure that a fair and impartial investigation is conducted.

CHAPTER 14

Gathering and Preserving Evidence

Introduction

Gathering and preserving evidence is a crucial step in any workplace investigation. The evidence collected can be used to determine the facts of the case, and it is important that this evidence is collected and preserved in a way that is reliable, accurate, and admissible in court.

Types of Evidence

There are several types of evidence that can be collected in a workplace investigation, including:

- Eyewitness statements
- Physical evidence
- Documentary evidence
- Electronic evidence
- Expert evidence

It is important to consider which types of evidence are relevant to the specific case and to gather as much evidence as possible.

For example, if the investigation is related to harassment or discrimination, eyewitness statements and physical evidence (e.g. emails, text messages, notes) may be particularly important. If the investigation is related to fraud or embezzlement, financial records and electronic evidence (e.g. computer logs, CCTV footage) may be key.

Gathering Evidence

Gathering evidence must be done in a way that is legal, ethical and respectful to all parties involved. It is important to use proper techniques when gathering evidence, such as interviewing witnesses, searching for documents, and analyzing electronic data. It is also important to ensure that the evidence is collected in a way that preserves its integrity and authenticity, for example, by taking photographs of physical evidence or making copies of electronic data.

Preservation of Evidence

Once the evidence has been collected, it is important to properly preserve it in order to ensure that it remains in the same condition as when it was collected. This may include storing physical evidence in a secure location, making copies of electronic evidence, and properly labeling and documenting all evidence.

It is also important to ensure that the chain of custody of the evidence is maintained, meaning that the evidence is handled by authorized personnel, and the movement and location of the evidence is documented.

Conclusion

Gathering and preserving evidence is a crucial step in any workplace investigation. The evidence collected can be used to determine the facts of the case, and it is important that this evidence is collected and preserved in a way that is reliable, accurate, and admissible in court. By taking the time to properly gather and preserve evidence, organizations can ensure that their investigation is thorough and that the evidence can be used to determine the facts of the case.

CHAPTER 15

Developing a Plan and Timeline for the Investigation

Introduction

Developing a plan and timeline for a workplace investigation is essential to ensure that the investigation is conducted in an efficient, thorough, and effective manner. A well-structured plan and timeline will help to keep the investigation on track, ensure that all relevant parties are informed, and that the investigation is completed in a timely manner.

Setting Objectives

The first step in developing a plan and timeline for the investigation is to establish the objectives of the investigation. This should include identifying the specific issues that the investigation is intended to address and the outcomes that are desired.

For example, the objectives of an investigation into harassment might include identifying the perpetrator, determining the extent of the harassment, and taking appropriate action to prevent future incidents.

Identifying Tasks and Responsibilities

Once the objectives of the investigation have been established, the next step is to identify the specific tasks and responsibilities required to achieve those objectives. This should include tasks such as interviewing witnesses, gathering evidence, and analyzing data.

It is also important to identify the key personnel who will be responsible for carrying out these tasks. This may include internal investigators, external consultants, or a combination of both.

Developing a Timeline

Once the tasks and responsibilities have been identified, it is important to develop a timeline for the investigation. This should include milestones for completing key tasks, such as interviewing key witnesses, and deadlines for completing the investigation.

The timeline should also include regular check-ins to ensure that the investigation is progressing as planned and that any unexpected issues are addressed in a timely manner.

Conclusion

Developing a plan and timeline for a workplace investigation is essential to ensure that the investigation is conducted in an efficient, thorough, and effective manner. By setting clear objectives, identifying tasks and responsibilities, and developing a timeline, organizations can ensure that the investigation is completed in a timely manner and that all relevant parties are informed throughout the process. This will help to build trust in the integrity of the investigation and maintain confidence in the organization.

CHAPTER 16

Interviewing Witnesses

Introduction

Interviewing witnesses is a critical step in any workplace investigation. The information obtained from witnesses can provide valuable insights into the events under investigation and can help to establish the facts of the case. However, it is important to conduct witness interviews in a professional and unbiased manner to ensure the integrity of the investigation.

Preparing for Interviews

Before conducting any witness interviews, it is important to prepare for the interviews by reviewing any relevant documentation, such as complaints or reports, and identifying any key issues or questions that need to be addressed. It is also important to provide any necessary background information to the interviewer, such as the purpose of the investigation and the specific issues that need to be addressed.

Conducting the Interviews

When conducting witness interviews, it is important to establish a comfortable and confidential environment. This can be done by conducting the interviews in a private location and informing the witness that their participation is voluntary and that they are free to leave at any time. The interviewer should also inform the witness of their rights and any potential consequences of providing false or misleading information.

During the interview, the interviewer should use open-ended questions to encourage the witness to provide detailed and candid responses. The interviewer should also be mindful of their own biases and avoid leading or suggestive questions. It is important to take detailed notes of the interview, including the witness's name, the date and time of the interview, and a summary of the witness's statements.

Follow-up and Confirming Information

After the interview, it may be necessary to follow-up with the witness to clarify or confirm information provided during the interview. It is important to document any follow-up communication in the same manner as the initial interview.

Conclusion

Interviewing witnesses is a critical step in any workplace investigation. By preparing for interviews, conducting them in a professional and unbiased manner, and following-up to confirm information, organizations can ensure that they gather accurate and reliable information from witnesses. This will help to establish the facts of the case and ensure that the investigation is conducted in a thorough and effective manner.

Interview Styles

- **Structured Interview**: This method follows a pre-determined set of questions and is typically used to gather specific information from a witness or suspect.

- **Unstructured Interview**: This method is less formal and is used to gather general information about a situation. It allows the interviewer to follow leads and explore new information as it arises.

- **Behavioural Interview**: This method focuses on a person's past behavior as a predictor of future behavior. It is used to gather information about how a person has handled similar situations in the past.

- **Cognitive Interview**: This method is used to improve the accuracy and completeness of a witness's memory by using techniques such as mental reinstatement and imagination.

- **Interview under oath**: This method is a formal interview conducted under oath, typically in front of a court reporter or video-recorder. This type of interview is often used in legal proceedings and can be used as evidence in court.

- **Confrontational Interview**: This method is used to challenge a witness or suspect's account of events by confronting them with contradictory evidence or inconsistencies in their statement.

- **Motivational Interview**: This method is used to help a witness or suspect understand the consequences of their actions and to encourage them to change their behavior.

- **Hypothetical Interview**: This method is used to explore a witness's or suspect's thoughts, feelings, and reactions to a hypothetical situation.

It's important to note that each of these styles has their own advantages and disadvantages, and it's important to choose the best method for the specific situation.

CHAPTER 17

Documenting the Investigation

Introduction

Proper documentation is a crucial component of any workplace investigation. It serves as a record of the investigation process, the evidence collected, and the findings of the investigation. It also helps to ensure that the investigation is conducted in a fair and unbiased manner, and can be used to defend any decisions or actions taken as a result of the investigation.

Types of Documents

Investigation Plan: An investigation plan should be developed and documented at the beginning of the investigation. It should include the scope of the investigation, the objectives, and the timeline for completion.

Interview Notes: Detailed notes should be taken during all witness interviews, including the witness's name, the date and time of the interview, and a summary of the witness's statements.

Evidence: All evidence collected during the investigation should be properly documented and preserved, including physical evidence and any documents or electronic files.

Investigation Report: A report summarizing the findings of the investigation should be prepared and include a summary of the evidence collected and the conclusions reached.

Retention and Confidentiality

All documentation related to the investigation should be kept confidential and stored in a secure location. Organizations should have a retention policy in place for how long the documentation will be kept on file.

Conclusion

Proper documentation is essential to ensure that workplace investigations are conducted in a fair and unbiased manner, and to defend any decisions or actions taken as a result of the investigation. By documenting the investigation plan, interview notes, evidence, and findings, organizations can ensure that all aspects of the investigation are recorded and can be reviewed as needed. Additionally, it is important to keep all documentation confidential and retain it according to the organization's policy.

CHAPTER 18

Evaluating Credibility and Evidence

Introduction

Evaluating the credibility of witnesses and the evidence collected during a workplace investigation is crucial to determining the truth of the matter and reaching accurate conclusions. This chapter will discuss the best practices for evaluating credibility and evidence in a workplace investigation.

Evaluating Witness Credibility

- **Look for consistency**: Compare what a witness says during the interview to what they have said in the past, or to what other witnesses have said.

- **Consider the witness's demeanor**: A witness's body language, tone of voice, and level of confidence can indicate whether they are telling the truth or not.

- **Assess the witness's bias**: Consider whether the witness may have a motive to lie or exaggerate.

- **Check for independent corroboration**: Verify the witness's statements with other evidence or testimony.

Evaluating Evidence

- **Verify the authenticity of the evidence**: Ensure that the evidence is what it purports to be and that it has not been tampered with.

- **Assess the relevance of the evidence**: Determine whether the evidence pertains to the issue being investigated.

- **Evaluate the probative value of the evidence**: Consider whether the evidence has any bearing on the conclusions of the investigation.

- **Assess the credibility of the evidence:** Consider the source of the evidence and whether it is reliable.

Conclusion

Evaluating the credibility of witnesses and the evidence collected during a workplace investigation is crucial to determining the truth of the matter and reaching accurate conclusions. By looking for consistency, considering the witness's demeanor, assessing the witness's bias, and checking for independent corroboration, investigators can evaluate the credibility of the witness. Additionally, by verifying the authenticity, assessing the relevance, evaluating the probative value and assessing the credibility of the evidence, investigators can evaluate the evidence and make fair and unbiased conclusions.

CHAPTER 19

Making Findings and Recommendations

Introduction
Making findings and recommendations is the final step in a workplace investigation. It is important to be thorough and objective when making findings and recommendations, as they will be used to make decisions about how to address the issues that were investigated. This chapter will discuss the best practices for making findings and recommendations in a workplace investigation.

Making Findings
- **Review all of the evidence**: Make sure that all of the evidence collected during the investigation has been considered when making findings.

- **Use a preponderance of the evidence standard**: Determine whether it is more likely than not that the allegations being investigated are true.

- **Be specific and clear**: Clearly state what the findings are and what evidence supports them.

- **Address all issues**: Make sure that all of the issues that were investigated are addressed in the findings.

Making Recommendations

- **Tailor recommendations to the specific situation**: Recommendations should be specific to the issues that were investigated and take into account the unique circumstances of the case.

- **Consider the impact on all parties:** Recommendations should take into account the impact that they will have on all parties involved, including the person who made the allegations, the person who is accused, and any other employees who may be affected.

- **Be realistic and practical**: Recommendations should be realistic and practical, taking into account the resources and limitations of the organization.

- **Address any systemic issues**: If the investigation has revealed any systemic issues within the organization, recommendations should address how to address and prevent these issues from occurring again in the future.

Conclusion

Making findings and recommendations is the final step in a workplace investigation. It is important to be thorough and objective when making findings and recommendations, as they will be used to make decisions about how to address the issues that were investigated. By reviewing all of the evidence, using a preponderance of the evidence standard, being specific and clear, and addressing all issues, investigators can make fair and unbiased findings. Additionally, by tailoring recommendations to the specific situation, considering the impact on all parties, being realistic and practical, and addressing any systemic issues, investigators can make effective and practical recommendations that address the issues that were investigated.

CHAPTER 20

Communicating the Findings to Stakeholders

Introduction
Communicating the findings of a workplace investigation is an important step in addressing the issues that were investigated. It is important to be clear, concise, and respectful when communicating the findings, as they will be used to make decisions about how to address the issues that were investigated. This chapter will discuss the best practices for communicating the findings of a workplace investigation to stakeholders.

Identifying Stakeholders
- **Determine who the stakeholders are**: Identify who will be affected by the findings of the investigation and who needs to be informed of the findings.

- **Consider internal and external stakeholders**: Stakeholders can include employees, management, the person who made the allegations, the person who is accused, and any outside parties, such as regulatory agencies or legal counsel.

Preparing the Communication
- **Be clear and concise**: Clearly and concisely state the findings and recommendations of the investigation.

- **Use non-legal language**: Use language that is easy for non-experts to understand.

- **Be respectful**: Be respectful and sensitive to the privacy and confidentiality of all parties involved.

- **Include next steps**: Clearly state any next steps that will be taken as a result of the findings and recommendations.

Delivering the Communication

- **Choose the appropriate medium**: Decide on the most appropriate medium for communicating the findings, such as a written report, email, or in-person meeting.

- **Use a neutral tone**: Use a neutral tone when communicating the findings to avoid any appearance of bias.

- **Allow for questions and feedback**: Allow stakeholders to ask questions and provide feedback on the findings and recommendations.

Conclusion

Communicating the findings of a workplace investigation is an important step in addressing the issues that were investigated. It is important to be clear, concise, and respectful when communicating the findings, as they will be used to make decisions about how to address the issues that were investigated. By identifying stakeholders, preparing the communication, delivering the communication, and allowing for questions and feedback, investigators can ensure that the findings of the investigation are clearly and effectively communicated to all stakeholders.

CHAPTER 21

Implementing Corrective Action

Introduction

Implementing corrective action is the final step in addressing the issues that were investigated during a workplace investigation. The goal of corrective action is to prevent the issue from happening again and to ensure that the workplace is a safe and respectful environment for all employees. This chapter will discuss the best practices for implementing corrective action following a workplace investigation.

Identifying Corrective Action

- **Review findings and recommendations**: Review the findings and recommendations of the investigation to determine what corrective action needs to be taken.

- **Identify appropriate corrective action**: Identify the appropriate corrective action that needs to be taken to address the issues that were investigated. This can include disciplinary action, policy changes, additional training, or other measures.

- **Assess feasibility and effectiveness**: Assess the feasibility and effectiveness of the proposed corrective action to ensure that it will address the issues that were investigated.

Implementing Corrective Action

- **Communicate corrective action to stakeholders**: Communicate the corrective action that will be taken to all stakeholders, including employees, management, and any outside parties.

- **Follow through on corrective action**: Follow through on the corrective action that was identified and ensure that it is fully implemented.

- **Monitor and evaluate**: Monitor and evaluate the effectiveness of the corrective action to ensure that it is addressing the issues that were investigated and preventing them from happening again.

Conclusion

Implementing corrective action is the final step in addressing the issues that were investigated during a workplace investigation. The goal of corrective action is to prevent the issue from happening again and to ensure that the workplace is a safe and respectful environment for all employees. By identifying appropriate corrective action, implementing it, and monitoring its effectiveness, investigators can ensure that the workplace is a safe and respectful environment for all employees.

CHAPTER 22

Documenting the Investigation and Maintaining Records

Introduction

Documenting the investigation and maintaining records is an important aspect of any workplace investigation. Proper documentation and record keeping helps ensure the integrity of the investigation, and it can also be used to support any actions that may be taken as a result of the investigation. This chapter will discuss best practices for documenting the investigation and maintaining records.

Documenting the Investigation

- **Create a case file**: Create a case file that contains all the relevant documents and information related to the investigation, including the complaint, witness statements, and any other relevant documents.

- **Document all actions**: Document all actions taken during the investigation, including the date, time, and details of each action taken.

- **Keep accurate notes**: Keep accurate notes of all interviews, meetings, and other actions taken during the investigation.

- **Document decisions and findings**: Document all decisions and findings made during the investigation, including any decisions to terminate or discipline employees.

Maintaining Records

- **Retention policy**: Implement a retention policy for all records related to the investigation. This should include guidelines for how long records should be kept and the process for destroying or disposing of records.

- **Secure storage**: Store all records related to the investigation in a secure location that is only accessible to authorized personnel.

- **Confidentiality**: Maintain the confidentiality of all records related to the investigation and ensure that only authorized personnel have access to them.

Conclusion

Proper documentation and record keeping is critical to the integrity of any workplace investigation. By creating a case file, documenting all actions taken during the investigation, keeping accurate notes, and maintaining records in a secure location, investigators can ensure that the investigation is conducted in a thorough and professional manner, and that any actions taken as a result of the investigation are supported by the evidence. It also helps to comply with the legal requirement for keeping records.

CHAPTER 23

Staying Current with Legal Developments

Introduction

Workplace investigations are subject to various federal and state laws and regulations, and it is important for investigators to stay current with these laws in order to conduct investigations that are compliant with legal requirements. This chapter will discuss best practices for staying current with legal developments in the area of workplace investigations.

Keeping Up-to-Date with Laws and Regulations

- **Research**: Research and stay informed about federal and state laws and regulations that pertain to workplace investigations, including discrimination, harassment, and whistleblower protection laws.

- **Legal updates**: Regularly review legal updates and stay informed about any changes to laws and regulations that may affect workplace investigations.

- **Consult with experts**: Consult with legal experts and other professionals who specialize in workplace investigations to stay informed about the latest legal developments.

Understanding Case Law

- **Reviewing court decisions**: Review court decisions that have been made in cases related to workplace investigations to stay informed about how the law is being applied in these cases.

- **Analyzing trends**: Analyze trends in court decisions to anticipate how the law may be applied in future cases.

- **Understanding precedents**: Understand the precedents that have been set in court decisions and how they may apply to your own investigations.

Conclusion

Staying current with legal developments is an essential aspect of conducting compliant workplace investigations. By researching and staying informed about federal and state laws and regulations, regularly reviewing legal updates, and consulting with experts, investigators can ensure that their investigations comply with legal requirements. Additionally, by staying informed about case law, investigators can better anticipate how the law may be applied in future cases, as well as understand how to apply legal precedents to their own investigations.

CHAPTER 24

Enhancing Investigation Skills

Introduction
Conducting effective and compliant workplace investigations requires a set of specialized skills. This chapter will discuss best practices for enhancing investigation skills in order to conduct investigations that are thorough, fair, and unbiased.

Professional Development

- **Training**: Attend training courses and workshops on workplace investigations, such as those offered by professional associations or legal organizations.

- **Reading**: Read books, articles, and other materials on workplace investigations, in order to stay informed about the latest techniques and best practices.

- **Mentorship**: Seek out experienced investigators who can provide guidance and mentorship in the field of workplace investigations.

Continual Learning
- **Staying informed**: Stay informed about the latest developments and best practices in workplace investigations by reading relevant publications, attending

conferences and seminars, and participating in webinars and other online training.

- **Reflecting on past investigations**: Reflect on past investigations and identify areas where your skills can be improved, such as interview techniques or evidence gathering.

- **Practicing**: Practice your skills through mock investigations or by observing experienced investigators in action.

Conclusion

Enhancing investigation skills is essential for conducting effective and compliant workplace investigations. By seeking out professional development opportunities, staying informed about the latest developments in the field, reflecting on past investigations, and practicing your skills, investigators can improve their ability to conduct thorough, fair, and unbiased investigations.

CHAPTER 25

Resources for Ongoing Learning and Development

Introduction
Conducting effective and compliant workplace investigations requires a commitment to ongoing learning and development. This chapter will provide a list of resources that can be used to stay informed about the latest developments and best practices in workplace investigations.

Professional Associations

- **National Employment Lawyers Association (NELA):** NELA is a professional association of attorneys who represent employees in discrimination, harassment, and other employment-related cases. NELA offers training and resources for attorneys who handle workplace investigations.
  https://www.nela.org/

- **Society for Human Resource Management (SHRM):** SHRM is a professional association for human resource professionals. SHRM offers training and resources on a wide range of topics related to workplace investigations, including legal compliance, best practices, and evidence gathering.
  https://www.shrm.org/

Legal Organizations

- **American Bar Association (ABA)**: The ABA is a professional organization for attorneys. The ABA offers training and resources on a wide range of topics related to workplace investigations, including legal compliance, best practices, and evidence gathering.
https://www.americanbar.org/

- **National Employment Law Institute (NELI)**: NELI is a professional organization that provides training and resources for attorneys and human resource professionals on a wide range of employment law topics, including workplace investigations.
https://www.neli.org/

Online Resources

- **Workplace investigations e-learning course**: This online course provides an overview of the key elements of workplace investigations, including legal compliance, best practices, and evidence gathering.
https://www.workplaceinvestigationscourse.com/

- **Workplace Investigations Blog**: This blog provides updates on the latest developments and best practices in workplace investigations, as well as case studies and other resources.
https://www.workplaceinvestigationsblog.com/

Conclusion

Staying informed about the latest developments and best practices in workplace investigations is essential for conducting effective and compliant investigations. The resources listed in this chapter, including professional associations, legal organizations, and online resources, can be used to enhance investigators' knowledge and skills and improve their ability to conduct thorough, fair, and unbiased investigations.

CHAPTER 26

Summary of Key Points

Legal Considerations:

An examination of the federal and state laws that govern workplace investigations, as well as best practices for compliance and common legal pitfalls to avoid.

Types of Workplace Investigations:

A discussion of different types of workplace investigations, such as those related to harassment and discrimination, fraud and embezzlement, workplace violence and threats, and ethical misconduct.

Planning and Preparation:

Information on how to identify the scope of an investigation, select investigators, gather and preserve evidence, and develop a plan and timeline for the investigation.

Conducting the Investigation:

Tips on interviewing witnesses, documenting the investigation, evaluating credibility and evidence, and making findings and recommendations.

Concluding the Investigation:

Information on communicating the findings to stakeholders, implementing corrective action, and documenting and maintaining records of the investigation.

Continuing Education and Professional Development:

A focus on staying current with legal developments, enhancing investigation skills, and resources for ongoing learning and development.

CHAPTER 27

Encouraging Ongoing Learning and Professional Development

As we wrap up this training book on workplace investigations, it's important to remember that this is just the beginning. The field of workplace investigations is constantly evolving, with new laws and best practices emerging all the time. In order to stay current and continue to improve your skills, it's essential to engage in ongoing learning and professional development.

One of the best ways to do this is by staying informed about developments in the field. This can be done through subscribing to relevant industry publications, attending conferences and seminars, or participating in online training programs. It's also a good idea to join professional organizations, such as the Association of Workplace Investigators, which provide access to a wealth of resources and networking opportunities.

Another key aspect of professional development is to continue to hone your investigation skills. This can be done by seeking out opportunities to conduct investigations in your workplace, or by volunteering to serve as an investigator for a professional organization. Additionally, practicing mock investigations with colleagues can be an effective way to build your skills and gain valuable feedback.

Lastly, it's important to remember that professional development is not just about gaining new knowledge, but also about reflecting on your own practice. Reflecting on past investigations and considering areas where you can improve is an essential part of ongoing learning and professional development.

Workplace investigations can be a challenging and rewarding field. By staying current with legal developments, enhancing your investigation skills, and engaging in ongoing learning and professional development, you will be well-equipped to conduct investigations that are fair, thorough, and respectful of all parties involved.

CHAPTER 28

Additional Assistance

As you have progressed through this training book, we hope that you have gained a better understanding of the complexities and nuances of workplace investigations. However, we understand that every situation is unique and that there may be times when you need additional guidance or support.

That's why we want to provide you with some contact information for further assistance.

First and foremost, your organization's human resources department should be your first point of contact. They are likely to have a wealth of knowledge and experience when it comes to workplace investigations and can provide you with the guidance and support that you need.

In addition to your HR department, there are also a number of professional organizations and resources that you can turn to for assistance. For example, the Society for Human Resource Management (SHRM) provides a wide range of resources and information on workplace investigations and other related topics. The Equal Employment Opportunity Commission (EEOC) also provides guidance on compliance with federal anti-discrimination laws.

You can also find a list of legal experts, investigators, and other professionals who specialize in workplace investigations. These experts can provide you with specialized support, such as conducting an investigation on your behalf or providing legal guidance.

We also recommend that you stay up-to-date with the latest developments in workplace investigations. This can be done by reading relevant books, articles, and online resources, or by attending seminars or webinars.

In summary, while this training book provides a comprehensive overview of workplace investigations, you may still have questions or need additional guidance. Remember that your organization's HR department and various professional organizations and resources are always available to assist you. And don't forget to continue your learning journey to stay current with the latest developments in this field.

OTHER RESOURCES

- "The Essential Guide to Workplace Investigations" by Lisa Guerin and Amy Delpo
- "Conducting Workplace Investigations: A Step-by-Step Guide" by Lisa Guerin and Sharon D. Nelson
- "Workplace Investigations: A Primer for Employers and Practitioners" by Michael J. Lotito and Lisa J. Banks
- "The Complete Guide to Workplace Investigations: Proven Strategies for Effectively Resolving Discrimination, Harassment, and Other Workplace Issues" by Carol Anne Buck
- "Conducting an Investigation: A Guide for Employers and Practitioners" by Society for Human Resource Management (SHRM)

These are just a few examples, and there are many other resources available on the topic, including online articles and videos, as well as in-person training courses and webinars.

Employee investigation training is typically conducted by organizations or companies, either through their own human resources department or by hiring a third-party consultant. Some examples of organizations that provide employee investigation training include:

- Human resources consulting firms
- Law firms that specialize in labor and employment law
- Professional associations or organizations, such as the Society for Human Resource Management (SHRM)
- Government agencies, such as the Equal Employment Opportunity Commission (EEOC)
- Professional development and training providers such as Dale Carnegie, Franklin Covey,etc.

I can also suggest some resources that you can use to access information on workplace investigation interview methods and styles:

- The Society for Human Resource Management (SHRM) website offers a variety of resources on workplace investigations, including information on different interview styles and techniques.
  https://www.shrm.org/resourcesandtools/tools-and-samples/hr-qa/pages/investigations.aspx

- The Equal Employment Opportunity Commission (EEOC) also provides guidance on conducting effective workplace investigations, including information on different interview methods.
  https://www.eeoc.gov/laws/guidance/investigations

- The Association of Workplace Investigators (AWI) is a professional organization that provides resources and training on workplace investigations, including information on different interview techniques. https://www.awi.org/

- The International Association of Interviewers (IAI) offers training and resources on various interview techniques, including those used in workplace investigations. https://www.certifiedinterviewer.org/

- The American Bar Association (ABA) provides guidance on workplace investigations, including information on different interview methods. https://www.americanbar.org/groups/litigation/resources/

- OSHA provides guidance on how to conduct an effective workplace investigation, including information on different interview methods. https://www.osha.gov/laws-regs/standardinterpretations/2019-11-08

- The National Employment Law Institute (NELI) provides training and resources on workplace investigations, including information on different interview techniques. https://www.neli.org/

- The American Society for Industrial Security (ASIS) offers guidance and resources on workplace investigations, including information on different interview methods. https://www.asisonline.org/Pages/default.aspx

- The International Association of Chiefs of Police (IACP) provides guidance and resources on workplace

investigations, including information on different interview techniques.
https://www.theiacp.org/

- The National White Collar Crime Center (NW3C) provides training and resources on workplace investigations, including information on different interview methods.
https://www.nw3c.org/

*Please note that some of these resources may require you to be a member or pay a fee to access some of the resources.

www.ingramcontent.com/pod-product-compliance
Lightning Source LLC
Chambersburg PA
CBHW071626040426
42452CB00009B/1506